W9-BNG-124

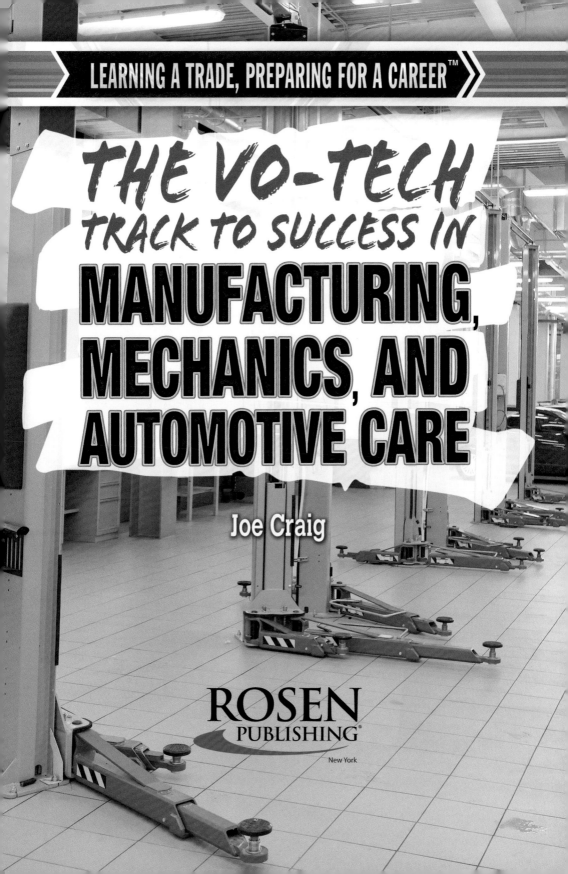

THE VO-TECH TRACK TO SUCCESS IN MANUFACTURING, MECHANICS, AND AUTOMOTIVE CARE

Joe Craig

ROSEN
PUBLISHING

New York

Published in 2015 by The Rosen Publishing Group, Inc.
29 East 21st Street, New York, NY 10010

Library of Congress Cataloging-in-Publication Data

Craig, Joe
The vo-tech track to success in manufacturing, mechanics, and automotive care/Joe Craig.—First edition.
    pages cm—(Learning a trade, preparing for a career)
Includes bibliographical references and index.
ISBN 978-1-4777-7734-3 (library bound)
1. Industrial arts—Vocational guidance—Juvenile literature. I. Title.
T56.3.C73 2015
670.71'1—dc23

2013049330

Manufactured in the United States of America

CONTENTS

INTRODUCTION

The majority of young men and women in the United States and Canada graduate high school and go to a four-year college. Those four years can be a time of great personal growth. They can broaden students' horizons considerably and give them the necessary tools to start their life as gainfully employed adults.

College is expensive, however. The price of four-year college tuition can keep the traditional college experience out of reach for many young men and women. Students who do not have much money or don't do well in a traditional academic setting might have a hard time gaining admission at a standard college. Furthermore, a lot of students just don't want to attend college. They don't want to continue their academic education and would rather start their careers quickly. Or perhaps they don't believe that a four-year degree program would get them any closer to their life goals. A traditional four-year college program is not for everyone.

These days, we're made to believe that a college degree is required for career success and financial stability. The truth is, though, that there are no guarantees. There are more college graduates today than ever, yet unemployment remains relatively high. Why are so many college-educated men and women unemployed? It's due to the fact that although their

Vo-tech programs allow students to get practical, hands-on training to start their careers early. A garage is the classroom for this automotive mechanics class.

college education was probably very beneficial in other ways, it did not prepare them for the contemporary workforce. In spite of their expensive education, some unemployed college graduates do not have the skills they need to get a job. At the same time, however, there are very few well-paying opportunities for a high school graduate who does not have special training.

This situation might make it seem like there are few viable options for those who seek a postsecondary (after high school) education. And it might seem like there aren't any options for young men and women who can't or don't want to go to college. But this is just not true. Students who forgo the traditional academic track can pursue vocational and technical education.

Vocational-technical, or vo-tech, high schools are institutions that teach practical skills for a certain vocation, or job. Career and technical education, or CTE, is a national vo-tech initiative. Vo-tech and CTE programs have the same goal, but they may attempt to accomplish it differently. Since the global recession of 2009, the U.S. and Canadian governments, along with the private sector, have pushed for increased CTE programs to lower unemployment and jump-start the economy. Proponents of CTE believe it makes financial and career security more attainable to students who wouldn't go to college anyway, whether by choice or because they are not in a financial or academic position to do so. Vo-tech and CTE are both forms of vocational and technical education that prepare students for a career. We'll use both terms in this book.

Traditional high school courses are valuable and important to every young person. However, they are not enough to get one started in a career. If students don't follow through and go to college after high school, their job opportunities will be severely limited. Vo-tech high schools give students hands-on training in their chosen career paths. However, young men and women can pursue vo-tech training even if they don't attend a special vo-tech high school. There are also postsecondary CTE programs.

CTE programs in manufacturing, mechanics, and automotive care are common. Manufacturing programs prepare students to enter the workforce as manufacturing production workers, logisticians, distributors, and managers. Mechanics and automotive care programs train students for work repairing and maintaining cars, vehicles, and machinery.

Manufacturing, mechanics, and automotive care careers are vital to the U.S. economy. This book will examine these industries and provide information about CTE programs in these career concentrations. The goal is to provide you with enough information to help you make an educated decision about your future. Learning manufacturing, mechanics, or automotive care skills, whether through high school vo-tech/CTE programs, postsecondary education, or both, is an excellent way to obtain a successful career and a higher standard of living at a cost that you can afford.

Chapter One

MAKE IT WORK!: MANUFACTURING

When you think of manufacturing, you might imagine cavernous factories with towering rows of automated machinery constructing cars or other objects that are equally massive, heavy, and metallic. It certainly can be that, but in actuality, "manufacturing" is a very general term. Manufacturing is simply the production of goods of all shapes and sizes.

The manufacturing sector creates a huge variety of goods—cars, microchips, processed foods, clothing, tools, cleaning supplies, industrial machinery, furniture, and much more. Literally anything that's made is manufactured. Even a carpenter building a one-of-a-kind table is producing a good and, therefore, manufacturing. Industrialization and mass production have reduced the economic importance of individual craft production, however. So for the purposes of this book, we will discuss only the production of goods on a large scale.

Advanced manufacturing techniques include computerized robots creating circuit boards and microchips. Consequently, skilled high-tech manufacturing workers are in serious demand.

Changes in the Manufacturing Industry

In recent years, manufacturing has accounted for almost $2 trillion, nearly 12 percent of the U.S. gross domestic product (GDP). The global recession of 2009 hurt the U.S. manufacturing sector, especially apparel and transportation manufacturing, which lost jobs to globalization. It's simply cheaper for manufacturing companies to open factories in developing nations. There, they can pay less in wages and overhead than in the United States or Canada. As a result, in 2010, China surpassed the United States as the world's largest manufacturer.

Domestic manufacturing has shown some recent renewed growth, however. The United States has added

This laborer works on a car's undercarriage. The global economic recession of 2009 hit the automotive manufacturing industry hard. Many employees were laid off.

manufacturing jobs in certain industries, like chemical manufacturing. Because the U.S. government has created new incentives to bolster the manufacturing job market, advanced manufacturing—or manufacturing that uses high-tech processes to create high-tech products—could potentially continue to grow. The White House has tried to level the playing field for American manufacturing by investing in research and development, reforming the tax code to make investment more attractive to business owners, and cracking down on unfair trade practices in countries like China.

Each different good that's manufactured provides a wide variety of career tracks that are accessible through vo-tech and CTE programs. In fact, manufacturing is one of the most common concentrations of vo-tech and CTE programs. This chapter will explore several manufacturing career tracks that apply to the majority of manufacturing processes: engineering and drafting; production; logistics and distribution; business, management, and administration; and maintenance, installation, and repair.

Engineering and Drafting

Before a factory can begin to produce a good, the laborers need to know what they are making. Knowing it is a leaf blower is not enough. What does it look like? How big is it? How does it work? What materials will be used? How do you put it together? That's where engineers and drafters come in.

Engineers use math, science, and creativity to conceive and design the goods that will be manufactured and plan the most efficient way to manufacture them. Engineers also solve the technical problems that might arise during manufacturing. It takes a unique combination of imagination and logic to be an effective engineer.

Engineers have to communicate their ideas in the clearest way possible. Drafters work with engineers, architects, and/or scientists to create technical drawings or blueprints. A technical drawing is a visual reference describing the size, shape, appearance, and function of an object. It provides a plan that explains how to manufacture the product. Drafters don't design the things they are drawing, but they must still be creative and able to accurately visualize products right down to their smallest parts. They also choose the materials to be used based on strength and cost. Drafters need to know technical terminology in order to communicate with engineers. They must be knowledgeable in math, especially geometry, and science.

Most engineering careers require at least a bachelor's degree. Many drafting jobs, however, are obtainable with vo-tech education and postsecondary vocational or on-the-job training. Certain drafting positions may require a two-year associate's degree.

Bicycles, fighter jets, sewer systems, and microwaves—engineers and drafters work together to design them all. Besides a mastery of math and science, they must have an expert knowledge of the things they are designing. There is too much for one person to know, and so engineers and drafters specialize in particular areas. An electronic drafter, for example, diagrams circuit boards. An aeronautical

Drafters must use complicated mathematics to make sure that their technical drawings are precise. Seemingly small mistakes can lead to big problems.

drafter draws airplanes, and an automotive drafter draws cars.

Drafters work on a project-by-project basis. If they are architectural or electrical drafters, they might make trips to a worksite to take measurements. Drafters used to draw by hand, but these days they spend most of their time in front of a computer. They must be meticulous—technical drawings can only serve their purpose if they're clear and precise. Drafters must have good communication skills and work well in groups. It's an excellent career path for a creative person who likes planning, solving problems, and figuring out how things work.

Production

Once engineers have designed a product and figured out the best way to produce it, and drafters have created the technical drawings, it is time to bring their plans to life. Production workers are the men and women who actually manufacture the goods. They're laborers, machine operators, and technicians.

It typically takes many production workers to build something, especially a product that is large and/or has lots of intricate parts. For this reason, production workers tend to have specialized roles within their chosen industry. For example, one laborer working in an automotive manufacturing plant might specialize in assembling electronic components for the dashboard display, while another might operate the machinery that fabricates the hood. These laborers would not do the same jobs if they were building washing machines, as those don't have dashboard displays or hoods. Although there are general skills that apply to all production jobs, each role in each factory requires different skill sets and experiences.

Production jobs usually require a high school diploma and some on-the-job training. High school vo-tech programs can give prospective manufacturing production workers an early start, with specially targeted courses and hands-on lessons.

Today, automotive manufacturing workers must use computers and robotics. Manufacturing jobs become more and more complex as technological advances rapidly redefine products and the way they're made.

Manufacturing production jobs become more sophisticated every day. Where laborers once built goods by hand, they now use cutting-edge tools and robotics. As a result, production jobs require more training than they once did. While that may seem to make it more difficult to start a career, it could also mean more job security for well-trained U.S. and Canadian production workers who have specialized knowledge. Potential CTE students

ASSEMBLY LINES

An assembly line, or progressive assembly, is a process in manufacturing in which many workers, each with his or her own specialty, build a product in sequential stages. No one worker completes the job from start to finish. Instead, the manufactured good passes from one laborer to another down a line. Each person focuses on assembling an individual part or section of the product. By the time the product reaches the final worker at the end of the line, it has been fully assembled.

Progressive assemblies have been widely used because they are typically more cost effective and efficient than having only a few people work on a product from step one through to completion. That's because assembly lines allow for more products to be worked on simultaneously. If there are twenty steps in an assembly line, a factory can work on twenty units at once.

Assembly lines are also cost effective because they allow for an efficient division of labor. This means that production workers need only partial, focused knowledge of the manufacturing process. That makes it easier to train workers. Before assembly lines became popular in the beginning of the twentieth century, goods were manufactured individually.

Assembly line work carries its own set of challenges. It can be monotonous and unsatisfying for laborers to work all day repeating the same actions. If you are interested in working in manufacturing production, you can expect to work in an assembly line. If you don't think you'd enjoy working on an assembly line, production work may not be right for you.

should do some research to make sure their courses are up to date with current equipment and the latest techniques.

Manufacturing laborers, machine operators, and technicians typically work in factories. Production workers should enjoy working with tools. They must work well with others because they work in teams, and they should be comfortable using computers and learning about new technology.

Logistics and Distribution

Once production workers have done their part, newly manufactured goods must be transported to customers. That is where logistics and distribution workers come in. Logistics and distribution workers move the manufactured product and coordinate those movements. They are truck drivers, warehouse stockers, shipping clerks, packagers, and forklift operators.

Without logistics and distribution workers, the manufactured product would never reach the customer. Instead, goods would gather dust on the factory floor, and that would mean a huge financial loss for the company. But there's more to it than that. The repercussions of a logistics and distribution stoppage could be a disaster for us all. Think of the many manufactured goods that are essential to our daily life. We need drugs and medical supplies, clothing, diapers, toilet paper, cooking oil, and gasoline (a precious commodity that affects the distribution of all other goods). What would we do without these essential commodities? We can thank logistics and distribution workers for making all of these things available to us every day.

Stockers, packagers, and forklift operators work in factories or warehouses. They organize, arrange, and prepare goods for shipment. Clerks work in offices, most likely on-site at the warehouse or factory, to plan and manage shipments. They maintain logs and paperwork to help keep track of goods. Clerks have to know where everything is at any given time. They also create delivery schedules and make sure logistics and distribution workers adhere to them. They need to be very organized, with supreme time-management skills.

Truck drivers pick up and deliver goods to the customer. Truck driver jobs are distinguished by the size of their load and the amount of time spent on the road. Interstate truck drivers, also known as over-the-road drivers, travel thousands of miles and are on the road for weeks at a time. Someone who is excited by a nomadic lifestyle traveling the country would do well as an interstate truck driver. The routes of delivery drivers, on the other hand, are usually confined within one city or region.

This forklift operator moves, organizes, and keeps track of manufactured goods in a warehouse. Truck drivers and other logistics and distribution workers will deliver these goods to the customer.

Logistics and distribution jobs usually require a high school diploma and on-the-job training. Truck drivers usually require special licenses, the particular one depending on the goods they are transporting and the size of their truck. Forklift operators need a special certification, too. Logistics and distribution workers should be able to prioritize, meet deadlines, and coordinate activities in spite of many scheduling and logistical conflicts.

Business, Management, and Administration

Business, management, and administration workers don't deal directly with the production of manufactured goods but with operating the manufacturing business. It takes many workers who are fulfilling many individual and interlocking responsibilities to make sure that a manufacturer's research and development, production, and distribution systems are all functioning properly. Bookkeepers, office clerks, customer service representatives, human resources specialists, and sales representatives are all vital to a company's existence. Without them, the company would never be able to manage its employees, serve its customers, or allocate finances for its daily operation.

The daily lives of business, management, and administration employees vary greatly, depending on their position. Each job requires a different set of traits and abilities.

Customer service representatives make sure that customers are satisfied. They are the face of the company. If a customer has any questions or grievances, he or she goes through customer service.

Sales representatives use their knowledge of the manufactured product to present it in an attractive and desirable way in an effort to persuade potential buyers. A manufacturing company needs talented sales

Customer service representatives answer customers' calls and e-mails. They must be courteous and helpful, or else the company's profits could suffer.

representatives or else it will have a difficult time making a profit, regardless of the product's quality.

Bookkeepers and accountants calculate and keep track of financial records. They have to be meticulous because accounting mistakes can cost a lot of money and can damage a business' reputation.

Human resources specialists hire new employees and manage the manufacturing company's existing workforce. They must be good with people, as a large part of their job is interacting with workers. They also have to address and resolve interpersonal conflicts among employees.

Business, management, and administration workers need skills that are not necessarily specific to manufacturing, but every position requires some basic knowledge of manufactured goods and processes. Sales representatives, for example, need to know what they are selling and what sets it apart from similar offerings from competitors. Business, management, and administration workers tend to work in offices. They use standard office equipment, such as computers, telephones, and fax machines. Most positions require a high school diploma and on-the-job training. Vo-tech/CTE programs may offer courses in manufacturing business, or they may just offer general business courses.

Chapter Two

GET UNDER THE HOOD: MECHANICS AND AUTOMOTIVE CARE

O ur society relies heavily on complicated vehicles and machines that the average person doesn't completely comprehend. We might know how to use a lawnmower or drive a car, but what do we do when a lawnmower or car breaks down? Most of us can't fix them ourselves, so we call a mechanic.

Mechanics repair and maintain vehicles and machinery. "Automotive care professional" is a more general term that refers to anyone who cares for any part of a car, not just the mechanical parts. By 2020, the demand for auto mechanics in the United States is expected to grow 17 percent over 2010 levels. Mechanics and automotive care courses are among the most common in vo-tech and CTE. In fact, there is a shortage of skilled mechanics and automotive care professionals in the United States and Canada.

Mechanics: Highly Skilled Workers

As vehicles and machines become more technologically advanced, it becomes increasingly difficult for the average person to maintain his or her own vehicles and appliances. Today, cars are more sophisticated than ever—they even have computers inside of them. Mechanics use special diagnostic tools to interface with these computers. These tools are inaccessible to the rest of us. In the future, we'll likely rely more and more on mechanics to maintain our cars, diagnose problems, and fix what is wrong.

Auto mechanics use computers, special software, and diagnostic tools to interface with modern cars' microprocessors and figure out what's wrong.

Automotive care professionals are different from automotive manufacturing workers. Automotive manufacturing laborers work on assembly lines to build cars. Automotive mechanics fix broken cars and perform routine maintenance. Mechanics are employed in the manufacturing sector, however, usually to repair tools and machinery. But they can, and do, work outside of manufacturing, too.

Mechanics and automotive care professionals tend to have a passion for vehicles and machinery, for fixing things, and for working with their hands and with tools. Mechanics and automotive care professionals must adapt to changing technology, keeping up with all advances in the field. They must be good at identifying and solving problems. Some mechanics and automotive care professionals must have good customer service skills, too.

There are specialized types of mechanics, at least one for every type of vehicle and machinery: automotive mechanics, auto body technicians, diesel mechanics, aircraft mechanics, industrial machinery mechanics, small engine mechanics, and so on.

Automotive Mechanics

Automotive mechanics use their detailed knowledge of cars and car parts to diagnose and fix automotive problems. They also perform routine maintenance, such as oil changes and tire rotations. Many auto mechanics work in repair shops, car dealerships, and car parts stores. For them, customer service skills are a must.

In addition to their technical know-how, automotive mechanics must have the ability to clearly communicate with customers and make them feel at ease.

The average driver doesn't understand how his or her car operates or why it's broken. Mechanics have to effectively communicate with customers. They have to use information from the car owner and computerized diagnostic tools to figure out what is wrong. Once they do, they must clearly explain the problem to the customer, how it can be fixed, and how much it will cost to do so. It is extremely important that an auto mechanic earns his or her customers' trust and makes them feel comfortable, especially if he or she wants return business. Having little or no mechanical knowledge, the average customer measures his or her experience with a mechanic based on the speed and cost of the repair (which a mechanic may not have control over), as well as the level of trust that a mechanic inspires.

Not every auto mechanic works in a repair shop. Auto mechanics service Humvees for the army and school buses for the school district. You might also find them maintaining a fleet of rental cars, delivery trucks, or taxicabs.

Auto mechanics must be mindful of state and federal safety and environmental laws. Exhaust systems must meet certain emissions standards to ensure that they won't pollute, for example. It is part of an auto mechanic's job to make sure that cars are safe and street legal.

Automotive mechanics specialize in cars, but there are even more focused specializations within the automotive mechanical field. Different car makes and models and different types of autos, like diesel trucks, work differently and require special knowledge and skills.

Students can obtain the necessary knowledge and skills to be an automotive mechanic in special vo-tech programs, in postsecondary education, or through on-the-job training. Automotive mechanic must enjoy working with cars, customers, computers, and tools. They also shouldn't be afraid of getting dirty.

ALTERNATIVE FUEL VEHICLES

Today's cars are a good deal more advanced than in the past. GPS and LCD dashboard displays have become commonplace. These technological advances require mechanics and automotive care workers to learn skills that they never needed before.

Increased public attention on global warming and rising gas prices has created a growing desire for new, alternative fuel sources. The U.S. Energy Information Administration (EIA) estimates that there are about 1.2 million alternative fuel vehicles in use in the United States and 2 million hybrids. These numbers are expected to climb in the years ahead.

Alternative fuel vehicles have new, different parts. New parts mean new problems, new solutions, and new protocols for maintenance. For example, ethanol—an increasingly common alternative fuel—is corrosive. Cars that use ethanol or some other biofuels instead of gasoline could suffer over time. That is a problem that gas-powered cars don't have.

Scientists continue to research new alternative fuel sources. Hydrogen-powered vehicles could be in our future. Mechanics can be certain that the things they are repairing will only get more sophisticated in the years ahead. Auto care professionals have to adapt to any and all advances in technology.

Auto Body Technicians

Auto body technicians repair and finish car bodies. They are different from auto mechanics because they are only concerned with the outside of a car, not its engine or the way it drives. Some mechanics and repair shops are trained to provide both services though, and it's beneficial for an auto care professional to have a general knowledge of both auto mechanics and auto body repair.

Auto body technicians might repaint a car, fix a broken bumper after a crash, or replace a broken windshield. They must know how to apply plastics and adhesives. They have to know how to weld. They also patch broken parts with fiberglass.

Auto body technicians can work to restore a damaged car to its previous appearance or change it altogether. Custom auto technicians take auto body repair to the extreme. They use their auto body talents and a whole lot of imagination to create mobile works

This auto body technician is repairing a windshield. Auto body technicians are different from auto mechanics because they work solely on the outside of a car.

of art. In fact, custom auto technicians must be artistic, and they often take art and design courses. Auto body CTE programs will likely focus only on the basics of auto body collision repair.

You can learn to be an auto body technician on the job, in vo-tech programs, or in postsecondary education. A student interested in becoming a custom auto technician will have to take his or her education further. Still, it's good to know what opportunities are available, no matter how far down the line.

Auto body technicians should enjoy working with cars, customers, and tools. They also need to be precise. The tiniest miscalculation can result in a lopsided disaster.

Aircraft Mechanics

Aircraft mechanics maintain and repair aircraft. It's a specialized position, different from automotive mechanics, for the obvious reason—aircraft are different from cars. Aircraft mechanics have to know about airplane engines, electrical instruments, wings, landing gear, propellers, and more.

Safety is the top concern for an aircraft mechanic, as mechanical failures are more likely to be catastrophic and result in multiple fatalities than would be the case if a car experienced mechanical failure. The Federal Aviation Administration (FAA) and Transport Canada are regulatory agencies in the United States and Canada, respectively, that set many requirements for aircraft functionality and routine maintenance. Aircraft mechanics must be well versed in these regulations and make sure that their aircraft are up to legal safety standards.

These aircraft mechanics are working on an engine. Aircraft mechanics often work in teams, due to the relative complexity of airplanes.

Aircraft mechanics may work for commercial airlines, the FAA itself, or the military. They must have a passion for airplanes. They need to understand the principals of flight. It's a good idea, and often necessary, for an aircraft mechanic to get a pilot's license. Aircraft mechanics have to be meticulous and detailed in their work.

CTE programs in aircraft mechanics are much more rare than automotive care programs, so it's common for aircraft mechanics to have some form of post-secondary education. There are a few vo-tech high schools that specialize in aircraft mechanics, however, such as Aviation Career and Technical High School in Long Island City, New York.

Industrial Machinery Mechanics

Industrial machinery mechanics repair heavy tools and machinery. They have to know about electrical circuitry, special diagnostic equipment, pneumatic and hydraulic systems, welding, and sheet metal work. They also need to know how to read blueprints and technical drawings of the tools and machinery that they are repairing.

Industrial machinery mechanics usually specialize in a type of equipment or in a particular industry. Literally every business that uses heavy tools and machinery will need a mechanic at some point, so there are many, many different potential areas of focus. Industrial machinery mechanics might work on cranes, forklifts, farm equipment, refrigerators,

Cranes need servicing, too. That's where industrial machinery mechanics come in. They specialize in repairing heavy tools and machinery, like construction equipment.

and a host of specialized machinery used for manufacturing.

Students can apply general mechanical knowledge learned from a CTE program to a career as an industrial machinery mechanic. But they will likely need on-the-job training, since it's impossible for a vo-tech program to account for every type of industrial machinery.

Small Engine Mechanics

Small engine mechanics maintain and repair machines and vehicles with relatively small engines, such as leaf blowers, chainsaws, motorcycles, and jet skis. Small engine mechanics tend to specialize in one category of vehicle or machine.

Small engine mechanics might work for a store or dealer fixing the products it sells. They could work for a hardware store repairing lawnmowers or a motorcycle dealership repairing motorcycles. This job is very similar to an auto mechanic's. Like automotive mechanics, small engine mechanics deal with gas-powered and electrical engines, but a small engine mechanics job is generally less stressful than being an automotive mechanic, since there is less money at stake, the engines are simpler, and customer demand is smaller and less urgent. Just like with automotive mechanics, small engine mechanics need good customer service skills. It is a good idea for a student interested in small engine mechanics to learn the basics of automotive mechanics, too, in order to be more versatile.

This small engine mechanic is repairing a motorcycle. He must use hand tools of a smaller, more appropriate size in order to fit into tight spaces.

Small engine mechanics use small hand tools that can fit into tiny spaces. Students who are interested in possibly becoming a small engine mechanic should keep in mind that motorcycle mechanics, jet-ski mechanics, motorboat mechanics, and those who service other small recreational vehicles might be busy only during the warmer times of the year.

CTE programs for small engine mechanics are not as common as those for automotive mechanics, but they are not completely rare either. If a student is interested in small engine mechanics but does not have access to a small engine vo-tech program, he or she could first learn basic mechanic skills and then follow through with small engine mechanics in postsecondary education or with on-the-job training.

Chapter Three

GO VO-TECH!: HIGH SCHOOL VO-TECH AND CTE PROGRAMS

V o-tech high schools are high schools that teach technical skills in a certain vocation, in this case manufacturing, mechanics, and automotive care. Vo-tech is also known as career and technical education (CTE). There are vo-tech and CTE high schools all over the United States and Canada.

Enrolling in a vo-tech program does not mean a student stops taking traditional academic classes. That's a good thing because a traditional academic education is extremely valuable to everyone, even those who don't want to be mathematicians or historians. Most vo-tech programs are part-time, which means that students spend half of their school schedule in a regular, traditional high school classroom. There, they take the usual academic subjects, like math, science, English, and history.

The other half of their school day is spent in vocational/technical classes, either in an actual classroom or in a lab or workshop. It is also possible that teachers of academic subjects in CTE programs will purposely construct lesson plans that place the

Vo-tech high schools and CTE programs often combine traditional academics, math, science, English, and history, with hands-on training in the program's focus.

academic subject within the context of the vo-tech program's focus. For example, a science teacher at an automotive mechanic program might teach the science of car aerodynamics instead of general physics.

Getting to Work Immediately

Vo-tech high schools have a much more concrete goal than traditional high schools: to give students practical skills to start their careers as soon as possible after graduation. Traditional high schools, on the other hand, provide students with a range of general instruction and the basic knowledge that they need to enter college, be well rounded, and have an array of professional options in the future.

Vo-tech gets students started early; their professional future is now. They learn things that they would otherwise not learn until after graduation during post-secondary education, apprenticeships, or on-the-job training. Students who earn diplomas from CTE schools usually have an easier time finding certain jobs than students with typical high school degrees because they already have some practical skills, work experience, and professional contacts. Through vo-tech, they gain a valuable head start.

A manufacturing, mechanics, or automotive care vo-tech program can be very beneficial to certain students, but will it be for you? First you must decide if it is the right fit for you. Do you already know what you want to do for a living? Are you interested in working with cars? How about airplanes? Or electronics? Would you like to focus on learning practical skills for a single occupation or general knowledge to give you more options but less specialized expertise? Do you prefer listening and discussing theoretical topics or working with your hands? What are your goals after high school? Do you expect to go to college?

If you don't plan to go to college and are interested in a manufacturing or mechanics career instead, CTE could be for you. Make sure to do your homework. Research vo-tech programs and potential careers to be certain that you're making the right decision.

Nothing is irreversible, but you have to make your educational and professional choices very carefully.

What to Expect from a Vo-Tech Program

High school vo-tech programs that offer manufacturing, mechanics, and automotive care courses usually combine classroom lessons—both in academics and in manufacturing, mechanics, and automotive care—with practical, hands-on education. Teachers expect CTE students to learn by doing. Mechanic vo-tech schools typically have machine shops where students can learn and practice their skills on actual cars, motorcycles, or whatever their particular focus is.

CTE emphasizes real experience. Some CTE programs take students to actual worksites so that they can get an accurate, realistic, and detailed understanding of a day in the life of a manufacturing laborer or auto

Students in CTE programs can expect to learn by doing. In CTE, practical experience is just as important as theoretical knowledge.

body technician. Many teens like this approach better than the traditional classroom lecture, but it certainly isn't for everyone.

Manufacturing or automotive care professionals with real-world work experience often teach classes in CTE high schools. This means that students are learning from someone who has done the job before and may still have contacts with professionals working in the field.

Manufacturing, mechanics, and automotive care vo-tech high schools vary greatly in programming and quality. Generally speaking, some high schools offer only broad introductory CTE classes in the basics of manufacturing or automotive care. You wouldn't necessarily learn enough from these classes to be an expert, but they would still give you the foundational skills that you would need to start your professional journey. Other CTE high schools offer more in-depth training in several specializations of mechanics and automotive care.

Most vo-tech high schools give traditional diplomas upon graduation. This means that although the education is different, the actual pieces of paper are equivalent. That's not a bad thing—having a traditional high school diploma can help you reorient your career focus in case you change your mind later. Some vo-tech schools also offer industry certifications in mechanics or manufacturing skills.

Depending on the school and the area of expertise, a high school vo-tech program could provide enough training for a graduate to get an entry-level job upon graduation. Job candidates with a high school diploma

Graduates of vo-tech and CTE programs have knowledge and experiences that typical high school graduates do not. That can make them more desirable as employees.

are often hired for auto mechanic and manufacturing labor positions. The special skills and experiences earned in a vo-tech high school would only make a job applicant more desirable.

However, no vo-tech or CTE high school can guarantee its graduates a job immediately after graduation, no matter how good the program is. You should be suspicious of any school or program that makes such promises. The job market is in constant flux, and no one knows how things will change. The main reason to enroll in a manufacturing, mechanics, or automotive care vo-tech program is not to get a job quickly and easily—though it could potentially increase your chances of doing so—but because it's what you want to learn and it's the kind of work you want to do in the future.

Choosing the Right School or Program

A high school education will set you on a path toward your future. It's very important to make sure that you make the proper decisions so that you head in the direction that's right for you. If you do choose to pursue vo-tech education in manufacturing, mechanics, or automotive care, it is your responsibility to get the most out of it and use it to launch yourself into your career as effectively as possible.

Once you've decided to follow the vo-tech track, you will have to decide where to go to school. First, see what options are available in your community. Your local high school might offer CTE courses, if not a whole concentration. There might also be a vo-tech charter school in your county that you can apply to or a private vo-tech school that is within your family's budget. Compare each school and program to see which best fits your needs and circumstances.

How do you decide? First, check the school's facilities. Are they up to date? Are they well maintained? Does the school's equipment conform to the current

PROFESSIONAL ADVICE

When seeking good information to make an important decision, such as whether or not to pursue CTE, it is a good idea to go straight to the source. In this instance, that means manufacturing, mechanics, and automotive care professionals.

Daniel Lehmkuhl, considered one of the best automotive technicians in the country, has represented the United States in international automotive technology competitions. "There's a lot of pressure to go to school, to get a four-year degree," said Lehmkuhl in the AOL Jobs article "Becoming the Best Mechanic in the World." "But it's not for everyone. We shouldn't emphasize so much the education that puts you in a white-collar job, but finding the best fit for each person. I don't think everyone's cut out for college."

Several supply chain professionals and logistics workers were asked what advice they would give students who are interested in entering the field. In the article, "Career Advice for Aspiring Supply Chain Professionals," Phil Harris, who has worked in the industry for forty-five years, said, "To a student who wants to work in the industry, I would advise him/her to build a basic communications skill set which involves good technical understanding, solid communications skills, and analytical ability." Another supply chain professional, Nick Tweardy, said in the same article, "Try to learn as much as possible about the industry and the applications that keep it running."

In the "Career Advice" article, Terri Danz, director of a logistics consulting firm, said, "Take advantage of opportunities to do internships, even if unpaid, in the field while attending school. While there are many excellent supply chain management programs available, and they use real-life scenarios and case studies to teach, there is no substitute for time spent in the field seeing how things really work."

industry standards? If you're not sure, contact a local mechanic or factory office and find out. It might seem odd to contact a stranger this way, but no doubt this person will be happy to help guide a young person who is interested in doing what he or she does.

Next, research the school's faculty. Are they trained teachers or do they have applicable professional work experience? Industry professionals will have anecdotes and experiences that teachers do not, but trained teachers are typically better at creating lesson plans and communicating ideas.

Is the vo-tech school public or private? If it is a private school, how much is the tuition? Are there hidden costs, such as classroom supplies, or is it all provided? Can your family afford it? If not, could you get financial assistance? Sometimes private schools offer scholarships for students whom they deem worthy.

Find out the CTE program's graduation rate and job placement percentage. These numbers don't paint the whole picture, but they give good insight into the school's competence. Is the program licensed and accredited?

If you are considering a vo-tech high school, research its facilities. Are they well kept? Does the school have the latest industry standard tools and technology?

Has it been well reviewed? Has it received many complaints? If it is a private school, check with consumer advocate organizations like the Better Business Bureau (www.bbb.org).

Guidance counselors are excellent resources, too. They can give you indispensible advice and information to point you in the right direction. Make a meeting with your current guidance counselor or the counselor at the school you're considering.

Keep in mind that your education isn't confined to a vo-tech high school program. You can also look for

These two young interns are learning how to tune a bicycle gearshift. Internships are typically unpaid, but many offer high school or college credit in addition to their valuable training.

manufacturing, mechanics, or automotive care internships and apprenticeships with local businesses. You might be able to find a factory or car dealership with on-the-job training programs that also offer high school credit. Many community colleges offer vocational and technical courses, and you may be able to take them for credit at nights or on weekends while attending high school. Your high school may also have a CTE partnership with a local community college, and your school day could involve courses in both schools.

Chapter Four

TAKING IT FURTHER: POSTSECONDARY TECHNICAL EDUCATION

Vo-tech high schools can prepare a student for a career in manufacturing, mechanics, or automotive care, but a vo-tech high school education is not always enough for certain jobs. If a student wants to be an aeronautical mechanic or work in a specialized manufacturing plant, he or she will need more training than a vo-tech high school can offer. Even if a diploma and a vo-tech education are enough to get an entry-level job, as with positions in manufacturing labor, students might want to pursue some form of additional education to learn more skills or zero in on a professional specialization that will lead to career advancement. The more a worker knows, the more valuable he or she is to an employer, the greater the job security, and the more fulfilling and better-paying the work.

Most employers expect that new entry-level employees will need some kind of on-the-job training. Employers will most likely not be opposed to providing introductory training. They hire hard-working people who are reliable and dedicated and who have the potential to learn on the job. However, employers won't hire workers who don't already have some basic knowledge of the job and the industry, no matter how responsible and hard-working they are. Employers set education requirements for their job openings. They only consider applicants who meet these requirements. The more technical and complicated the position, the higher the education prerequisites.

Many manufacturing and automotive care jobs require on-the-job training. This can make vo-tech graduates more attractive employees, since they already have some applicable knowledge and experience.

When a High School Diploma Is Not Enough

If a high school diploma is not enough to get you the job you want, there are countless options available to get the necessary education. Community colleges sometimes offer relevant courses for manufacturing, mechanics, and automotive care careers. Unlike public CTE high schools, community colleges require that students pay tuition, although tuition is relatively inexpensive compared to state and private colleges. There are also technical and trade colleges. Like vo-tech and CTE high schools, technical colleges specialize in vocational and job-specific training, only on the postsecondary, or college, level. Community college and technical college postsecondary vo-tech programs usually require two years or less to complete. Some cities have adult education centers that offer CTE

This student is exhibiting his welding skills at the Annual Career and College Fest in Tampa, Florida. Festivals or conventions like this one are good places to get information.

courses and training in manufacturing, mechanics, and automotive care.

As you research potential postsecondary vo-tech programs, keep in mind that each has its own price and admission requirements. They're usually not too strict, but check and make sure that you meet the admission requirements, or you could be disappointed.

Also keep in mind that local car dealers and manufacturing companies sometimes sponsor vo-tech programs in technical colleges. Businesses may use their sponsored programs as ways to vet and recruit new employees.

So you've graduated high school. You know what career you want to pursue, and you know that you must continue your vo-tech education to do it. You've looked into the various options for a postsecondary vo-tech education near you. Now how do you decide where to go?

Accreditations

You've probably seen ads on TV for technical colleges. As more and more people look for training to get ahead in a competitive economy, postsecondary vocational and technical education has become a lucrative business. Private technical colleges are competing for your money. It is a big investment of your money and time, so it's in your best interest to research schools thoroughly. But how do you know if a technical school is legitimate?

You should do your best to find out as much as you can about the school you're planning to attend. Look up schools online and try to find news stories about them, positive or negative. Also find out whether or not a technical school is accredited.

Accreditation is the process by which a community college or technical training program is certified as being competent. When a school is accredited, it means that a trusted third-party group—in this case, an accrediting agency—has vouched for the school's professionalism. Accreditation is like a trusted friend telling you, "Don't worry, this guy is OK." It is a big red flag if a school is not accredited, and you should avoid unaccredited institutions at all costs. You can check the U.S. Department of Education's Database of Accredited Postsecondary Institutions and Programs at http://www.ope.ed.gov/accreditation/agencies.aspx. But how do you know if an accrediting agency is legitimate? Technical colleges can also receive certifications from industry unions or consumer groups, such as AAA.

Keep in mind that even if a school is accredited by a reputable organization, each accrediting agency has its own unique set of standards. One accrediting agency may not accept what another accrediting agency reports. To further complicate things, accrediting agencies have different jurisdictions. They can work internationally, nationally, or regionally. This means that if a student begins taking classes in a regionally accredited technical college and then transfers to a similar program at a nationally accredited technical college, credits might not transfer with that student.

As an added bonus, some technical colleges offer professional certifications in different skills and specializations within manufacturing, mechanics, or automotive

The U.S. Department of Education maintains the Database of Accredited Postsecondary Institutions and Programs. The database is available at http://www.ope.ed.gov/accreditation/agencies.aspx.

care. For example, students of an automotive mechanic program at a technical college can graduate with a certification for a certain car make, making it much easier to get a job. As you research postsecondary vo-tech and CTE programs, look for accredited schools that offer professional certifications. These certifications will tell future customers and prospective employers that you have been well trained, are highly skilled, and can be trusted.

No matter what you decide to do, always do your research. Don't ever take a technical school's claims at face value.

LABOR UNIONS

Labor unions are organizations of workers in the same industry that team up to reach common goals, such as better working conditions or higher pay. Labor unions elect leaders to bargain with employers on the union's behalf. These negotiations result in labor contracts that determine the rules of conduct for both sides.

Labor unions became popular during the Industrial Revolution, when many employers held all the cards and mistreated their workers in the name of greater profits. Laborers united, or unionized, to regain bargaining power and leverage. It is easy for an employer to ignore a few workers, but what can he or she do when the entire workforce stands up together? Many employers tried to fight back, and some even resorted to violence. But labor unions stuck around, and employers had no choice but to invite them to the bargaining table.

Labor unions are often seen as being at odds with business interests. As a result, they are not always politically popular, but they are often the only effective and influential advocates for workers' rights.

You may want to consider researching a labor union in your chosen field. As a member of a union, you may be able to gain access to job resources, special training, health insurance, and a pension fund, not to mention professional camaraderie and friendship with colleagues. Find out what the union in your industry offers. If you're interested in joining, see what you need to do to begin the process of gaining membership. The Aircraft Mechanics Fraternal Association, the United Automobile Workers, the International Longshore and Warehouse Union, and the International Brotherhood of Electrical Workers are just a few examples of strong and influential unions responsible for skilled workers in various industries.

Unions advocate for workers' rights and quality of life. These members of the United Automobile Workers are showing their support for more investment in their local auto plants.

Financial Aid

Unlike public vo-tech high schools, technical colleges and most other forms of postsecondary education, public and private, require that students pay tuition. Public technical colleges receive the majority of their funding from the state and federal government. Public technical colleges are significantly cheaper than private technical colleges, which are operated by companies or private organizations. The average cost of a two-year degree from a public college is $2,451, while the same degree costs an average of $11,480 at a private college.

Even if you go to a public school, a postsecondary vo-tech education is a serious investment. When a student enrolls in a postsecondary vo-tech program, he or she is likely old enough to be legally considered an adult and old enough to join the workforce. But committing to a postsecondary technical education that will expand future career options means that the student may lose out on work experience and a salary in the present. That loss of employable hours and compensation is a hidden cost of a postsecondary vo-tech education.

Thankfully, there is financial aid. Financial aid is funding from a third party that is used to help students pay for school and school-related expenses, such as tools, supplies, materials, books, and student housing.

Financial aid is both merit-based and need-based, and it comes in the form of scholarships, grants, and student loans. Merit-based financial aid is awarded to

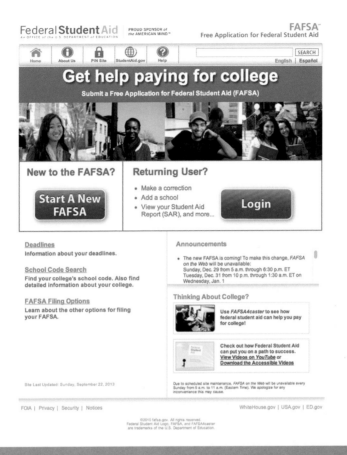

The U.S. government uses the FAFSA to decide whether or not a student will receive federal financial aid. You can fill it out and file it at https://fafsa.ed.gov.

students based on their abilities and achievements. For example, a student could win merit-based financial aid by getting a high score on the SATs, good grades in coursework, and/or performing many hours of community service. Need-based financial aid is given to a student based on how much money his or her family has. It operates on the idea that financial aid should go to those who need it the most. Scholarships and grants are financial awards that do not need to be repaid. Student loans are borrowed money and must be repaid over time, with interest.

U.S. students looking for financial aid should fill out the FAFSA, or Free Application for Federal Student Aid. The FAFSA is used to determine if a student is eligible for federal financial aid. The federal government offers its own grants, scholarships, and loans to U.S. citizens based on their financial need. It is a good idea for students to complete the FAFSA even if they don't expect to receive federal aid. This is because some independent scholarships and grants also use the FAFSA to determine whether or not a student is deserving of financial aid.

Chapter Five

EMBRACE THE FUTURE!: TECHNOLOGICAL ADVANCES AND LIFELONG LEARNING

Cars are getting more technically complex every day. In fact, new autos come off the assembly line with as many as fifty built-in microprocessors. These tiny computers help precisely control a car's engine so that it meets federal emissions standards. The microprocessors also monitor the car while it's on the road in order to manage the vehicle's traction and stability. With these new technologies, automobiles are getting "smarter."

New technology exists to make things safer, more convenient, and more comfortable for drivers. In some ways, the technology can make things easier for mechanics, too. For example, a car's many microprocessors actually help mechanics diagnose and solve problems. They do that by keeping track of any mechanical failures. When the owner brings his or her car in for service, the mechanic plugs in a diagnostic computer. The microprocessors then let the diagnostic computer know what's wrong.

These new innovations also make the practice of car mechanics more complex. It's more difficult than ever for the average person to repair his or her car without professional training and equipment. The more

Automobile computer diagnosis is a relatively new advancement in automotive diagnostic technology. Auto mechanics must constantly be aware of and adapt to new technologies.

difficult it is, the less people will do it. Drivers will have to rely on professional and highly trained auto mechanics more and more.

Always Be Learning!

Mechanics and automotive care professionals have to learn more and more and stay up to date so that they can deal with cars' new complexities. It can be difficult for some to make the transition to more high-tech vehicle maintenance and repair. Only ten years ago, mechanics rarely had to work with computers. Now computer skills are central to the profession.

It doesn't stop there. Technology is advancing at a rapid pace, and there are many even more exciting things on the horizon. Cars that communicate with each other, airbags that stop cars before a crash, and cars that drive and park themselves—it's not only possible in our future, but it's actually likely to happen.

Technological innovations have affected, and will continue to affect, all vehicles and machinery and the mechanics who repair them. For example, rising fuel prices have pushed commercial airlines to use their imaginations to develop new "green" airplanes. Scientists and engineers are conducting further research and creating designs that could completely revolutionize the way we fly.

At the same time, commercial airlines like Virgin have taken steps toward developing passenger space travel. Customers will be able to pay to be taken into Earth's orbit and then brought safely back down. If aircraft mechanics don't keep up with the times and the evolving technology that goes into manufacturing, maintaining, and repairing the vehicles and machinery, they could suffer.

With the recent technological advances in the automotive and aerospace industries and with those that are sure to come, mechanics and automotive care professionals must continue to adapt and learn new skills. An automotive or aircraft mechanic with up-to-date

This is the Virgin Galactic SpaceShipTwo. Virgin is developing commercial space travel. Such technological advances and changes in the industry will affect aircraft mechanics in the future.

knowledge of the latest technologies will always have a competitive edge over slower-to-adapt peers.

Adapting to Tomorrow's Technology Today

Manufacturing workers are even more entwined with technological advances than are mechanics and automotive care professionals. That's because professionals in the manufacturing world must face high-tech changes on

ATOMICALLY PRECISE MANUFACTURING

Atomically precise manufacturing, or APM, is making products with, literally, atomic precision. APM involves bonding individual atoms together. It is a level of control unprecedented in human manufacturing. Currently, APM is only theoretical, but it is receiving billions of dollars in scientific research in order to make it a reality. That's because the potential for atomically precise manufacturing is enormous.

With APM, goods of a much higher quality could be produced much more efficiently and affordably, and with more readily available, less expensive materials like nitrogen, carbon, and oxygen. Think of what that would mean for the manufacturing sector. Manufacturing companies could make anything they want. They would no longer have to worry about obtaining raw materials, since they could use cheap alternatives. Nor would they have to worry about wasting raw materials during production. As Eric Drexler, an APM engineer and researcher, said, APM is like a factory in a box. If, or when, this technology comes to pass, we will be able to make anything we've ever wanted but could never find a practical way to create.

two fronts: with the goods they produce and with the machinery, tools, and techniques they use to produce them. New products, new tools, and new ways to produce old products—it can all dramatically change a manufacturing professional's job.

Think of smartphones, for example. In only a matter of years, they've become extremely common and are viewed as indispensible tools for daily living. And yet, as common as they are, they are also complicated

This quality control worker is checking a smartphone. The relatively new, wide demand for smartphones has created many advanced manufacturing jobs.

computerized devices. Smartphones have become a booming business. Every tech company wants to cash in, and they all have a smartphone model of their own. Though smartphones are not typically produced in North America, they have shaken up the advanced manufacturing industry. Most smartphones are produced overseas, but there are many plants in the United States and Canada that produce smartphone microprocessors. Most of those manufacturing jobs didn't exist until the first decade of the twenty-first century. Not only that, but the entire product and its manufacturing process were completely new.

High-tech and advanced manufacturing is especially attractive to corporations, governments, and the general public because jobs in advanced manufacturing pay very well compared to jobs in other types of manufacturing. And the industry is growing at a fast pace. Countries are investing in research and infrastructure to manufacture new technologies and stay competitive. If they can get in front of the changing trends, so to speak, they can stand to improve their economies significantly.

The technological advances on the horizon will certainly change the way goods are manufactured, but those changes could prove to be more dramatic than anyone ever imagined. Take additive manufacturing, also known as 3-D printing, for example. Special printers lay down thin layers of a material, one layer at a time, to create a 3-D object from a digital model. Like magic, 3-D printers seemingly create something from nothing. What could this mean for the future of manufacturing? If 3-D printers become household items, then the average person could print small objects whenever he or she wants. That could lead to a decline in demand for some manufactured goods. These printers could also change manufacturing processes, making it easier to produce certain parts when they're needed. Will 3-D printers become commonplace one day? There is no way to know for sure.

One thing we do know is that technology will become increasingly sophisticated and will continue to impact every aspect of society. It can be overwhelming, but it's not a bad thing. No one could have ever imagined how the Internet would impact our daily lives. The Internet

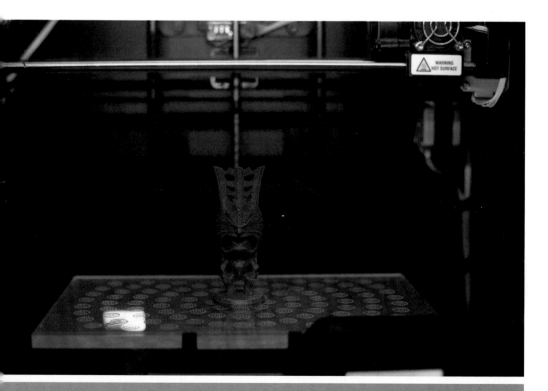

This red figurine was made by a 3-D printer. These printers use digital plans and instructions to make three-dimensional objects. This technology could change manufacturing forever.

has changed things forever, and it has created countless opportunities in the process.

It will be the same in the future. Change is inevitable. It's important that the manufacturing, mechanics, and automotive care professionals of the future recognize what is on the horizon, adapt to change, and search for opportunities that exist within new technologies. New technologies always open doors for new career specializations.

The Outlook for Tomorrow

The United States is one of the world's top manufacturers. It used to be the number one manufacturer in the world, though, without peer. Due to growing global competition, the economic recession of 2009, and changing trade agreements, the U.S. manufacturing sector has lost many jobs and China has taken the United States' position at the top. However, the United States is retaining—and even gaining—new, more highly skilled, and better-paying manufacturing jobs.

The U.S. government has invested in manufacturing with the hopes of kick-starting the troubled economy. President Barack Obama has repeatedly discussed the importance of manufacturing to the U.S. economy. In 2009, shortly after he was elected, the president approved an $80 billion government bailout of Chrysler and General Motors, the world's largest automaker as of 2012. In 2011, President Obama created the Advanced Manufacturing Partnership Steering Committee. In 2012, this committee released a report containing sixteen recommendations for how to "secure U.S. leadership in the emerging technologies that will create high-quality manufacturing jobs and enhance America's global competitiveness." This certainly shows the federal government's commitment to the future of manufacturing in America.

Still, there are no guarantees. It's always a good idea for manufacturing, mechanic, and automotive care workers to keep their skills sharp and pay attention to the economic and scientific trends that will affect their livelihoods. Governments and businesses in America and Canada are encouraging CTE as a solution for a lack of skilled workers and the lagging economy. It remains to be seen whether students will follow their lead and the supply of qualified and skilled workers will catch up with the demand.

Remember that education doesn't end when you get a job. Education is for life. It's never too late to learn something new, and it's never a bad thing. As you go forward on your journey into the workforce, remember to never neglect an opportunity to increase and expand your skills. By learning everything there is to know about your job and staying up to date on the latest trends and technologies, you will be making yourself extremely valuable to any employer in need of a smart, highly skilled, hard worker who knows exactly how to do the job and do it well.

Glossary

accreditation A third-party certification of something or someone as competent.

alternative fuel A material other than fossil fuel, coal, propane, or natural gas that can be used as fuel.

assembly line A process in manufacturing in which many workers, each with his or her own specialty, build a product in sequential stages; also known as progressive assembly.

auto body technician A professional who repairs and maintains car exteriors.

automotive care professional Anyone who cares for cars for a living. Automotive mechanics and auto body technicians are both automotive care professionals.

business, management, and administration The branch of the manufacturing career track that is concerned with operating a manufacturing business.

career and technical education (CTE) A form of vocational and technical education that prepares students for a particular job.

custom auto body technician An auto body technician who drastically alters the external appearance of a car.

division of labor A production process in which workers on a team each have individual tasks and specializations.

drafter A worker who creates technical drawings and blueprints.

engineer A professional who uses math and science skills to design goods and manufacturing processes.

grant A financial aid award that does not need to be repaid.

logistics and distribution The manufacturing career branch concerned with moving products and coordinating those movements.

manufacturing The production of goods for sale.

mechanic A person who repairs and maintains vehicles and machinery.

postsecondary education An education that comes after high school.

production The career branch of manufacturing that is concerned with the actual creation of goods.

scholarship A financial aid award that is given based on a student's need or merit. Scholarships do not need to be repaid.

technical drawing A visual reference that describes the size, shape, appearance, and function of an object and provides a plan to produce it.

vocational-technical (vo-tech) education An education that prepares students for a particular job or trade.

For More Information

Association for Career and Technical Education (ACTE)
P.O. Box 758621
Baltimore, MD 21275-8621
(800) 826-9972
Website: https://www.acteonline.org
The ACTE is the nation's largest nonprofit organization aimed at supporting and fostering technical
   education programs. It provides information
   to educators, technical education faculty,
   and legislators to help support the growth of
   more technical education programs across
   the country.

Canadian Auto Workers Union (CAW)
205 Placer Court
Toronto, ON M2H 3H9
Canada
(416) 497-4110 (ext. 6555)
(800) 268-5763 (ext. 6555)
Website: http://www.caw.ca
The Canadian Auto Workers Union is a labor union for
   workers of many different industries, including vehicle manufacturing.

Canadian Vocational Association (CVA)
c/o Ms. Jane Louks
P.O. Box 816
Ottawa, ON K0A 2Z0
Canada
(613) 838-3244
Website: http://www.cva-acfp.org

The CVA is a nonprofit organization dedicated to supporting vocational educators and assistants, as well as raising public awareness regarding the benefits of vocational institutions.

United Auto Workers (UAW)
8000 East Jefferson Avenue
Detroit, MI 48214
(800) 243-8829
Website: http://www.uaw.org
The UAW is made up of over 750 unions and provides support to both current and retired union members in the automotive, aerospace, and agricultural industries. It negotiates and lobbies for union workers' rights.

U.S. Department of Education
400 Maryland Avenue SW
Washington, DC 20202
(800) 872-5327
Website: http://www.ed.gov
The Department of Education works to further education for all U.S. students. Among other things, it collects and interprets data on schools and works to fight discrimination in education.

U.S. Department of Labor
200 Constitution Avenue NW
Washington, DC 20210
(866) 487-2365
Website: http://www.dol.gov

The Department of Labor oversees labor laws in the United States to ensure that workers' rights are being respected. It also maintains fair collective bargaining agreements and helps citizens find work.

Websites

Due to the changing nature of Internet links, Rosen Publishing has developed an online list of websites related to the subject of this book. This site is updated regularly. Please use this link to access the list:

http://www.rosenlinks.com/TRADE/Manuf

For Further Reading

Abrams, Dennis. *The Invention of the Moving Assembly Line: A Revolution in Manufacturing* (Milestones in American History). New York, NY: Chelsea House, 2011.

Billy, Cynthia A. *Career and Technical Education* (Issues That Concern You). Farmington Hills, MI: Greenhaven Press, 2013.

Borg, Kevin L. *Auto Mechanics: Technology and Expertise in Twentieth-Century America* (Studies in Industry and Society). Baltimore, MD: Johns Hopkins University Press, 2010.

Burill, Dan, and Jeffrey Zurschmeide. *How to Fabricate Automotive Fiberglass & Carbon Fiber Parts.* Minnesota, MN: S-A Design, 2012.

Candela, Tony. *Automotive Wiring and Electrical Systems.* Minnesota, MN: S-A Design, 2009.

Carmichael, L. E. *Hybrid and Electric Vehicles* (Innovative Technologies). Minneapolis, MN: Essential Library, 2013.

Clipston, Amy. *Roadside Assistance.* Grand Rapids, MI: Zondervan, 2011.

Cohn, Jessica. *Manufacturing and Transportation.* New York, NY: Facts On File, 2008.

Crawford, Matthew B. *Shop Class as Soulcraft: An Inquiry into the Value of Work.* New York, NY: Penguin Press, 2009.

Ferguson Publishing. *Automotives* (Ferguson's Careers in Focus). New York, NY: Ferguson Publishing, 2009.

Gray, Kenneth Carter. *Getting Real: Helping Teens Find Their Future.* Thousand Oaks, CA: Corwin, 2008.

Hansen, Courtney. *The Garage Girl's Guide to Everything You Need to Know About Your Car.* Nashville, TN: Cumberland House Publishing, 2007.

Joseph, Matt. *Automotive Sheet Metal Forming & Fabrication.* Minnesota, MN: S-A Design, 2011.

Kemp, Adam. *The Makerspace Workbench: Tools, Technologies, and Techniques for Making.* Sebastopol, CA: O'Reilly & Associates Incorporated, 2013.

Marlowe, Christine. *Car Mechanic.* Broomall, PA: Mason Crest, 2013.

Bibliography

Better Business Bureau. "Vocational and Propri-
etary Schools." 2013. Retrieved November 2013
(http://www.newyork.bbb.org/vocational-and
-proprietary-schools).

Deloitte.com. "Top 10 Nations Ranked by the 2013
Index." 2013. Retrieved October 2013 (http://
www.deloitte.com).

Federal Trade Commission. "Choosing a Vocational
School." August 2012. Retrieved November
2013 (http://www.consumer.ftc.gov/articles/
0241-choosing-vocational-school).

Gordon, Claire. "Becoming the Best Mechanic in the
World." AOL Jobs, October 5, 2011. Retrieved
November 2013 (http://jobs.aol.com/articles/
2011/10/05/becoming-the-best-mechanic-in
-the-world).

Gordon, Howard R. D. *The History and Growth of
Career and Technical Education in America.* Long
Grove, IL: Waveland Press, 2007.

Green, Kimberly A., and Richard C. Hinckley. *The
Career Pathways Effect.* Waco, TX: CORD Communications, 2013.

iSeek.org. "Careers in Manufacturing." 2013.
Retrieved October 2013 (http://www.iseek.org/
industry/manufacturing/careers/careers.html).

Jacobson, Kinga N. *Best Practices and Strategies for
Career and Technical Education and Training: A Ref-
erence Guide for New Instructors.* Bloomington, IN:
AuthorHouse, 2013.

Jan, Tracy, and Bryan Bender. "Auto Bailout in '09
Key to Obama's Survival in Ohio." *Boston Globe,*

October 30, 2012. Retrieved November 2013 (http://www.bostonglobe.com).

Kingkade, Tyler. "High School Vocational Education on the Upswing, Coaxing Students Away from Traditional Colleges." Huffington Post, March 18, 2013. Retrieved October 2013 (http://www .huffingtonpost.com/2013/03/18/high -school-vocational-education_n_2900169.html).

Koten, John. "What's Hot in Manufacturing Technology." *Wall Street Journal*, June 10, 2013. Retrieved November 2013 (http://online.wsj.com/news/ articles/SB10001424127887323855804578510 743894302344).

Manufacturing.gov. "About the Advanced Manufacturing Partnership 2.0." Retrieved October 2013 (http://www.manufacturing.gov/amp.html).

Martinage, Bernard M. *Apprentice Work: Vo-Tech Standards.* Seattle, WA: CreateSpace, 2013.

Nice, Karim. "How Car Computers Work." How Stuff Works. Retrieved November 2013 (http://auto .howstuffworks.com/under-the-hood/trends -innovations/car-computer.htm).

NYC Department of Education. "Career and Technical Education." 2013. Retrieved October 2013 (http://schools.nyc.gov/ChoicesEnrollment/CTE/ default.htm).

Paulden, Jack. "I Am a Commercial Truck Driver in the U.S. What Do You Want to Know?" *Guardian*, July 11, 2013. Retrieved November 2013 (http:// www.theguardian.com/commentisfree/2013/ jul/11/truck-driver-salary-life-on-road).

Plumer, Brad. "The U.S. May Have More Manufacturing Jobs Than We Think." *Washington Post*, September 5, 2013. Retrieved October 2013 (http://www.washingtonpost.com/blogs/wonkblog).

School Soup. "Automotive Mechanics Career Information." Retrieved November 2013 (http://www.schoolsoup.com/careers/career_info.php?career_id=170).

Science Daily. "Solving Ethanol's Corrosion Problem May Help Speed the Biofuel to Market." October 1, 2013. Retrieved October 2013 (http://www.sciencedaily.com/releases/2013/10/131001115736.htm).

Scott, John L., and Michelle Sarkees-Wircenski. *Overview of Career and Technical Education.* Orland Park, IL: American Technical Publishers, 2008.

Sirkin, Harold L. "To Ease the Skills Shortage, Bring Back the Vocational High School." *Bloomberg Businessweek*, March 20, 2013. Retrieved November 2013 (http://www.businessweek.com/articles/2013-03-20/to-ease-the-skills-shortage-bring-back-the-vocational-high-school).

State of Washington Office of Superintendent of Public Instruction. "Why CTE?" Retrieved October 2013 (http://www.k12.wa.us/CareerTechEd/WhyCTE.aspx#1).

U.S. Energy Information Administration. "How Many Alternative Fuel and Hybrid Vehicles Are There in the U.S.?" May 16, 2013. Retrieved October 2013 (http://www.eia.gov/tools/faqs/faq.cfm?id=93&t=4).

Wang, Victor C. X. *Definitive Readings in the History, Philosophy, Theories, and Practice of Career and*

Technical Education. Hershey, PA: Information Science Reference, 2010.

Wang, Victor C. X., and Kathleen P. King. *Building Workforce Competencies in Career and Technical Education.* Charlotte, NC: Information Age Publishing, 2008.

Wial, Howard. "How to Save U.S. Manufacturing Jobs." CNN, February 23, 2012. Retrieved November 2013 (http://money.cnn.com/2012/02/23/news/economy/manufacturing_jobs).

Woodyard, Chris. "Serious Shortage of Skilled Auto Mechanics Looming." *USA Today*, August 30, 2012. Retrieved October 2013 (http://usatoday30.usatoday.com/money/autos/story/2012-08-28/shortage-of-auto-mechanics-looms/57414464/1).

Index

About the Author

Joe Craig is a writer who lives in Queens, New York. He has previously written on issues relating to technology, engineering, public policy, contributing to society, and life planning. This is his fourth book for Rosen Publishing.

Photo Credits

Cover (mechanic) wavebreakmedia/Shutterstock.com; cover (background), pp. 1, 3 Vereshchagin Dmitry/Shutterstock.com; p. 5 Chris Schmidt/E+/Getty Images; p. 9 Matthew Borkoski Photography/Photolibrary/Getty Images; pp. 10, 60, 64 Bloomberg/Getty Images; p. 13 Jonathan Heger/E+/Getty Images; p. 15 Monty Rakusen/Cultura/Getty Images; p. 19 Dmitry Kalinovsky/Shutterstock.com; p. 21 dotshock/Shutterstock.com; p. 24 kurhan/Shutterstock.com; p. 26 michaeljung/Shutterstock.com; pp. 29, 34, 47 Goodluz/Shutterstock.com; p. 31 Patrik Stollarz/AFP/Getty Images; pp. 32, 45, 53 © AP Images; p. 36 Echo/Cultura/Getty Images; p. 38 Peter Muller/Cultura/Getty Images; p. 40 bikeriderlondon/Shutterstock.com; p. 44 Jacques LOIC/Photononstop/Getty Images; p. 48 © Cherie Diez/Tampa Bay Times/ZUMA Press; p. 58 gilaxia/E+/Getty Images; p. 62 © Khampha Bouaphanh/MCT/ZUMA Press; cover and interior elements alekup/Shutterstock.com (technical illustration), Jirsak/Shutterstock.com (tablet frame), schab/Shutterstock.com (text highlighting), nikifiva/Shutterstock.com (stripe textures), Zfoto/Shutterstock.com (abstract curves); back cover graphics ramcreations/Shutterstock.com, vectorlib.com/Shutterstock.com (gear icon).

Designer: Michael Moy; Photo Researcher: Karen Huang